# jewish wisdom

## —A JOURNAL—

### EDWARD HOFFMAN

CHRONICLE BOOKS

SAN FRANCISCO

## RELATED WORKS BY EDWARD HOFFMAN

*Opening the Inner Gates: New Paths in Kabbalah and Psychology*
*Sparks of Light: Counseling in the Hasidic Tradition*
*The Heavenly Ladder: Kabbalistic Techniques of Inner Growth*
*The Hebrew Alphabet: A Mystical Journey*
*The Kabbalah Deck: Pathway to the Soul*
*The Way of Splendor: Jewish Mysticism and Modern Psychology*

10 9 8 7 6 5 4 3 2 1

PRINTED IN HONG KONG

DISTRIBUTED IN CANADA BY
RAINCOAST BOOKS
9050 SHAUGHNESSY STREET
VANCOUVER, B.C. V6P 6E5

CHRONICLE BOOKS LLC
85 SECOND STREET
SAN FRANCISCO, CA 94105
WWW.CHRONICLEBOOKS.COM

DESIGN: HENRY QUIROGA
TYPESET IN OMNIA AND MRS. EAVES

ISBN: 0-8118-2982-0

*To the Memory of My Grandparents*

JEWS HAVE ALWAYS BEEN KNOWN AS "THE PEOPLE OF THE BOOK". Dating far back to antiquity, the Hebrew Bible was canonized during Roman occupation of the Holy Land. Yet, even in our new millennium, it remains the foundation for Judaism, Christianity, and Islam. The destruction of the Second Temple of Jerusalem led to the Diaspora, scattering the Jewish people throughout the world. As a result, the study of Scripture and the commentary based on it—together broadly known as Torah—became a sacred activity, preserving Judaism.

The Mishnah, the first compilation of Jewish law, appeared in the third century, including the guide for self-mastery known as *Pirke Avot* ("Ethics of the Fathers"). Jewish life elevated the written word and its exposition as a key pathway to spirituality, even to God. According to rabbinic lore, the Torah contained the secrets of the universe; paradise itself was depicted as a dazzling realm where the righteous expanded their knowledge of the Torah's supernal mysteries.

With such an outlook, the sages increasingly strove to promote Torah study for the young. Rabbi Judah ha-Nasi, who led Jewish affairs in the Land of Israel during the middle decades of the third century, sought to perfect elementary education by organizing schools in every town and village. Maintaining that the entire world is sustained by the breath of schoolchildren, he forbade their Torah study to be interrupted, even if the Temple of Jerusalem were to be miraculously rebuilt.

Over the ensuing centuries, subsequent interpretations of Scripture involving legal give-and-take based on the Mishnah, as well as homilies, legend, myth, folk sayings, and even humor coalesced into the multi-volume body of writing known as the Talmud. Organized in two separate versions—one in Jerusalem and the more important in Babylonia—the Talmud spurred additional Jewish writing, especially of a philosophical and moralistic nature.

At the dawn of the second millennium, diary-keeping decisively entered Jewish tradition and literature. The impetus seems to have been foreign travel. Among the first such books to ignite the Jewish imagination was the travel journal of Eldad ha-Dani, who appeared in Kairouan in the year 890 C.E. with detailed accounts of independent Jewish kingdoms in East Africa, Arabia, Khazaria, and Persia. Claiming to have found the ten lost tribes, ha-Dani liberally mingled legend with fact, thereby buttressing Jewish survivalist hope for many centuries.

The most famous Jewish travel diary was Benjamin of Tudela's twelfth-century account of his visits to Southern Europe and the East. Providing an eyewitness report of life in many lands, Benjamin's diary fascinated his contemporaries. From the thirteenth century onward, journals devoted to Holy Land trips comprised a considerable body of Jewish literature. While many of these merely offered conventional descriptions of holy places, others contained fascinating nuggets of information.

For instance, in his diary entitled *These Are the Events,* Jacob of Paris recorded the anomaly that he was sent to the Land of Israel to raise money for a Paris yeshiva (Jewish seminary). Jacob also provided vivid descriptions of Jewish life in Damascus and Baghdad. Likewise, the diarist Isaac Hilo of fourteenth-century Provence noted in his journal while visiting the Holy Land that many Jewish scholars from France and Germany had emigrated to Haifa, that the Jews of Acco were quite rich, and that those in Jaffa had a fine library.

Beginning in the European Renaissance, the act of journaling gained a prominent role in Jewish mysticism, known as Kabbalah (from the Hebrew root-word meaning "to receive"). No longer offering impersonal, floridly allegorical images of heavenly scenes, practitioners began describing their actual meditative experiences in their journals. Some of these works came to be circulated privately among Kabbalistic circles in Spain, Italy, the Holy Land, and neighboring areas; others were later published for even wider dissemination.

For instance, Rabbi Isaac of Acco in the late thirteenth century kept a diary called *The Book of Visions,* in which he described powerful, transcendental experiences including visitations from celestial beings. Likewise during the Renaissance, *The Book of Radiance,* written in Spain by Rabbi Joseph ha-Kohen, vividly presented his mystical perceptions while in trance-like states of consciousness.

Among the most important of all Kabbalists was Abraham Abulafia of thirteenth-century Spain. As the originator of a powerful meditative system—which he called "knowing God through the twenty-two letters of the Hebrew alphabet"—Abulafia exerted tremendous influence on Jewish spiritual practice through the present. Abulafia's detailed diaries recounted his precise meditative experiences utilizing Hebrew letters, chants, and yogalike body postures with altered forms of breathing. His writings served to guide Jews throughout the Mediterranean world interested in attaining higher awareness.

During the sixteenth century, the town of Safed in the Holy Land became the nexus for a tremendous flowering of Jewish mysticism. Many of its leading figures, revered to this day for their wisdom, avidly kept diaries to record their spiritual experiences. Although Rabbi Isaac Luria, the most influential Kabbalist of all, seemingly wrote no such works, his chief disciple and scribe, Rabbi Chaim Vital, certainly did so. Particularly intriguing for seekers today is the dream journal that Rabbi Vital kept for many years.

Perhaps even more fascinating is the lifelong diary through which Rabbi Joseph Karo presented the esoteric teachings he "heard" inwardly while in lofty states of consciousness. Celebrated for his erudition in codifying existing Jewish law, Rabbi Karo for decades underwent trances in which he would speak in an altered voice on such evocative themes as the higher nature of dreams, the right way to meditate, the nature of the deity, and even life after death and reincarnation. Following these discourses, which Rabbi Karo and his circle attributed to a spirit-guide (known in Hebrew as a *maggid*), he would record them in his diary. Though most of its many volumes have long since disappeared, fragments have survived for contemporary study.

Hasidism, the influential movement of Jewish renewal that arose in eighteenth-century Eastern Europe, specifically aimed to elevate each person's daily living. The term *hasid* means "devout" in Hebrew, and Israel ben Eliezer was the movement's charismatic, dynamic lay leader. Known as the Baal Shem Tov ("Bearer of the Good Name") because he was believed to possess mystical knowledge and power, he taught that many paths to holiness exist—not merely Talmudic study. Life is meant to be joyful and exalted, the Baal Shem insisted, declaring that, "Without the feeling of love, stimulated by pleasures, it is difficult to feel true love of God."

Several years before his death, the Baal Shem carefully chose and trained disciples who would succeed him in expanding the Hasidic movement. Consistent with his message, they utilized music, dance, story-telling, innovative meditative practices, and spiritual counseling to help Jews gain a greater closeness to the divine. Not only did such Hasidic luminaries as Rabbi Nachman of Bratslav (great-grandson of the Baal Shem) encourage journaling as a valuable activity, they actively kept their own journals. As one disciple recalled of Rabbi Nachman, "When the Rebbe was speaking before God, petitions and supplications would pour forth from his heart, and he would often bring up some particularly good argument, or compose an especially fitting and well-ordered prayer. He would take the prayers he particularly liked and preserve them in writing. These he would repeat many times."

Rabbi Nachman also maintained the time-honored Kabbalistic practice of recording his dreams in a journal. In keeping with his view that travel is often beneficial spiritually for instilling a fresh outlook on life, Rabbi Nachman traveled widely for his time and documented his experiences in his journal.

The early Hasidic leaders recommended journaling as a valuable tool for self-reflection and *teshuvah* (repentance, literally "returning to the Source"). Specifically, they encouraged Jews to record their musings regarding the Torah portion of the week and the symbolic meaning of the various holidays in their personal lives. In the Hasidic tradition, the monthly periods before Rosh Hashanah and Passover were viewed as particularly important times for such self-examination.

Throughout the modern era, Hasidism has continued to regard diaries with favor. For example, Rabbi Joseph Schneersohn, the sixth Rebbe of the worldwide Hasidic group known as the Lubavitchers, kept a meticulous diary for virtually his entire life. Courageously safeguarding Jewish learning in Russia during Stalin's brutal dictatorship, Rabbi Schneersohn escaped to the United States at the onset of World War II, where he began rebuilding Hasidism in a vastly different milieu. Especially after the war, Rabbi Schneersohn maintained a voluminous correspondence with Hasidism dispersed around the globe. He drew frequently from his own journals to offer advice, inspiration, hope, and encouragement.

Certainly, as "People of the Book," it's no accident that many Jews during the Holocaust relied upon diary-keeping for spiritual stability and nourishment. Some were as ordinary as thirteen-year-old Anne Frank, hiding with her family in an Amsterdam factory garret. Others were as erudite as psychiatrist Viktor Frankl, whose monumental post-war memoir *Man's Search for Meaning* originated in diary scraps written while he was an inmate at Auschwitz. Yet, common to all such Jews facing the unspeakable was their intuitive awareness that writing—especially soul-baring and keen witnessing—was ultimately redemptive for themselves, and for the entire world.

Today, our needs for Jewish sustenance are no less intense, but they exist in a time of unprecedented possibility for personal growth. Whether your preference is to record the outer events—seemingly small or large—of daily life, or to narrate your travels, describe your dreams and musings, meditations and prayers, or to relate inspiring teachings from books and conversations, this journal awaits your participation.

Whatever form of self-expression feels most comfortable to you, know that the act of journaling links your soul to a wonderful tradition of discovery, meaning, and wisdom.

*"Look to God, and be radiant."*

—————

PSALMS

> *"Every journey has a secret
> destination of which the traveler
> is unaware."*
>
> ——
>
> MARTIN BUBER

*"If everybody pulled in the same direction, the whole world would fall down."*

YIDDISH APHORISM

*"Whoever does not see God in every place does not see God in any place."*

RABBI MENACHEM
MENDEL OF KOTZK

"*There are two things it is
forbidden to worry about:
that which it is possible to fix,
and that which it
is impossible to fix. What is
possible to fix: fix
it, and why worry? What is
impossible to fix,
how will worrying help?*"

RABBI YECHIEL MICHAL
OF ZLOTCHOV

*"There are no rules when it comes to worshipping God, including this one."*

RABBI JACOB ISAAC,
"THE HOLY JEW"
OF PSHISKE

*"Who is wise? One who learns from all persons."*

BEN ZOMA

"From every human being, there rises a light that reaches straight to the heaven. And when two souls that are destined to be together find each other, their streams of light flow together, and a single brighter light goes forth from their united being."

THE BAAL SHEM TOV

*"God does not do the same thing twice. Each person shall know and consider that in one's qualities, one is unique in the world, and that none exactly alike ever existed."*

RABBI NACHMAN OF
BRATSLAV

"To find God means to find the way without end."

MARTIN BUBER

*"One of the most important goals
which you can set yourself
to achieve is the realization of God's
presence in your life."*

———

TEHILLA LICHTENSTEIN

*"The days pass and are gone, and one finds that he never really had time to think. One who does not meditate cannot have wisdom."*

RABBI NACHMAN OF
BRATSLAV

*"A dream uninterpreted is like a letter unopened."*

———

THE ZOHAR

*"Do not worry about tomorrow, because you do not even know what may happen to you today."*

YIDDISH PROVERB

"At every hour, the heavenly gates are open, and all those who wish to enter, may enter."

THE MIDRASH

*"Charity (tzedakah) from the heart leads to study from the heart."*

———

THE BAAL SHEM TOV

*"Teshuvah (repentance) does not involve creating anything new, but rediscovering the goodness that was always there."*

RABBI MENACHEM
MENDEL SCHNEERSON

"It is better that we look inside ourselves and see what is going on in here, than to look to the heavens, to see what is going on up there."

RABBI SHALOM
SHACHNA OF
PROHOBITZ

"Before praying, remember any good qualities you have, or any good deeds you have performed. This will put life into you and enable you to pray from the heart."

RABBI NACHMAN OF BRATSLAV

*"Do you desire that people love you?
Love them first."*

RABBI LEVI ISAAC OF
BERDICHEV

*"There is no Torah without wisdom, and there is no wisdom without Torah."*

THE ZOHAR

*"Let the honor of your friend be as dear to you as your own."*

PIRKE AVOT
(THE ETHICS OF THE
FATHERS)

*"There are only two ways to live your life. One is as though nothing is a miracle. The other is as though everything is."*

ALBERT EINSTEIN

*"A wise person hears one word and understands two."*

———

Yiddish proverb

"*Each person is bound to everyone else, and no one is counted separately.*"

RABBI MOSES CHAIM
LUZZATTO

*"One should respect the secret within the soul of every person."*

MARTIN BUBER

*"Better one deed than a thousand sighs."*

RABBI SHOLOM DOVBER
OF LUBAVITCH

*"Give of yourself…you can always give something, even if it is only kindness…No one has ever become poor from giving."*

ANNE FRANK

*"Remember that life is a celebration
or can be a celebration.
One of the most important things is
to teach man how to celebrate."*

RABBI ABRAHAM
JOSHUA HESCHEL

# SOURCES

**Baal Shem Tov.** "Master of the Good Name", the popular appellation of Israel ben Eliezer, the charismatic Hasidic founder of the mid-eighteenth century.

**Ben Zoma.** An outstanding scholar and mystic who lived in the Holy Land during the second century C.E.

**Buber, Martin.** A major Jewish philosopher of the twentieth century, he was born in Germany and immigrated to the Holy Land. His outlook was strongly influenced by Hasidism and mysticism.

**Einstein, Albert.** Acclaimed for his Nobel-Prize winning theories of space, time, and energy, the German-born Einstein was also an active figure on behalf of world Jewry.

**Frank, Anne.** A Jewish-German teenager famous for her posthumously published diary, written while she was hiding with her family in Nazi-ruled Amsterdam.

**Heschel, Abraham Joshua, Rabbi.** Among the greatest Jewish theologians of the twentieth century, he was born in Poland and immigrated to the United States after World War II. Rabbi Heschel taught ethics and mysticism at the Conservative movement's Jewish Theological Seminary in New York.

**Jacob Isaac, Rabbi ("The Holy Jew") of Pshiskhe.** An early Hasidic leader revered for his faith and devotion to Judaism.

**Lichtenstein, Tehilla.** Born in Jerusalem at the turn of the twentieth century, she immigrated in her youth to the United States, where she co-founded the Society of Jewish Science with her husband, Rabbi Morris Lichtenstein.

**Luzzatto, Moses Chaim, Rabbi.** A leading eighteenth-century Italian Kabbalist. His book *Derech Hashem* ("The Way of God") is still studied throughout the world today.

**Menachem Mendel of Kotzk, Rabbi.** A Hasidic founder well known for his emphasis on asceticism and solitude as means for spiritual development.

**Midrash.** The Jewish legendary tradition, originating in written form by Talmudic sages in the Land of Israel and in Babylonia.

**Nachman of Bratslav, Rabbi.** An early Hasidic leader famous for his mystical tales; the great-grandson of the Baal Shem Tov.

**Pirke Avot.** *The Ethics of the Fathers.* Appearing in the early third century C.E., it is a sacred collection of aphorisms regarding daily conduct; attributed to early Jewish sages.

**Psalms.** One of the books of the Hebrew Bible, attributed by traditionalists to King David.

**Schneerson, Menachem Mendel, Rabbi.** The seventh rebbe (spiritual leader) of the Lubavitcher Hasidim (1902–1994), he directed the group's phenomenal post–World War II growth in the United States and abroad.

**Shalom Shachna of Prohobitz, Rabbi (d. 1805).** An early Hasidic leader who emphasized joy in daily life.

**Sholom DovBer of Lubavitch, Rabbi (1860–1920).** The fifth rebbe of the Lubavitchers, he established schools for formal Hasidic study.

**Yechiel Michal of Zlotchov, Rabbi.** A companion of the Baal Shem Tov who was celebrated for his piety.

**Yiddish.** The secular language spoken by European Jewry, beginning around the ninth century in western Germany. Following the widespread migration of Jews eastward in the fourteenth and fifteenth centuries, Yiddish became heavily influenced by Slavic languages. By the sixteenth century, Yiddish writings began to appear.

**Zohar.** *The Book of Splendor,* which first appeared in late thirteenth-century Spain. It is the "bible" of Kabbalah and its most influential work. Ascribed to Shimon bar Yochai of the second century by traditionalists, scholars today attribute it to Moses de Leon, who is said to have composed most of it in the 1280s and 1290s.

# REFERENCES

*A Mystical Journey through the Hebrew Alphabet.* VHS video. Written by Edward Hoffman, illustrated and produced by Harvey Gitlin. Commack, New York: Four Worlds Press, 1989: POB 695, Commack, New York 11725. http://www.fourworldspress.com

Buber, Martin. *Tales of the Hasidim, Books One and Two.* Translated by Olga Marx. New York: Schocken, 1991.

Buber, Martin. *The Tales of Rabbi Nachman.* Translated by Maurice Friedman. New York: Avon, 1970.

*Ethics of the Fathers.* Translated by Philip Blackman. New York: Judaica Press, 1964.

Gribetz, Jessica. *Wise Words, Jewish Thought and Stories through the Ages.* New York: Morrow, 1997.

Hoffman, Edward. *The Hebrew Alphabet: A Mystical Journey.* San Francisco: Chronicle Books, 1998.

Hoffman, Edward (Editor). *Opening the Inner Gates: New Paths in Kabbalah and Psychology,* 2nd edition, Commack, New York: Four Worlds Press, 1998: POB 695, Commack, New York 11725. http://www.fourworldspress.com

Hoffman, Edward. *The Heavenly Ladder: Kabbalistic Techniques for Inner Growth.* Commack, New York: Four Worlds Press, 1998: POB 695, Commack, New York 11725. http://www.fourworldspress.com

Isaacs, Ronald H. *Words for the Soul: Jewish Wisdom for Life's Journey.* Northvale, New Jersey: Jason Aronson, 1996.

Klagsbrun, Francine. *Voices of Wisdom: Jewish Ideals and Ethics for Everyday Living.* New York: Pantheon, 1980.

Newman, Louis. *Hasidic Anthology.* New York: Schocken, 1975.

Schwartz, Leo W. (Editor). *Memoirs of My People. Jewish Self-Portraits from the 11th to the 20th Century.* New York: Schocken, 1963.

Schwartz, Howard. *Gabriel's Palace.* Oxford University Press, 1993.

Schneerson, Menachem Mendel. *Toward A Meaningful Life: The Wisdom of the Rebbe.* Adapted by Simon Jacobson. New York: Morrow, 1995.

Schneerson, Menachem Mendel. *Letters by the Lubavitcher Rebbe, volume 1, Tishrei–Adar.* Brooklyn: Kehot Publication Society, 1978.

Telushkin, Joseph. *Jewish Wisdom: Ethical, Spiritual, and Historical Lessons from the Great Works and Thinkers.* New York: Morrow, 1994.

Umansky, Ellen M. and Ashton, Dianne (Editors). *Four Centuries of Jewish Women's Spirituality.* Boston: Beacon, 1992.

*Zohar, volumes 1–5.* Translated by Harry Sperling and Maurice Simon. London: Soncino Press, 1931–1934.

## acknowledgements

This book would not exist without the valuable help of others. I'm grateful to Debra Lande, Senior Editor at Chronicle Books, for her initial and sustained enthusiasm throughout my effort. It's been truly delightful working with her. Editorial Assistants Jodi Davis and Carey Jones have been consistently helpful. I'm also indebted to Associate Editor Alan Rapp for first introducing my Judaica work to his colleagues at Chronicle Books.

I wish to thank Sara Axel, Harvey Gitlin, Cantor Bruce Halev, Aaron Hostyk, Rabbi Neal Kaunfer, Paul Palnik, Rabbi Steve Rosman, and Rabbi Rami Shapiro for their many stimulating conversations on the subject of Jewish spirituality: its essence over the course of history and its application today. Their encouragement, warmth, and insights are very much appreciated.

To all of the above, as well as to my Judaica teachers and students over the years—and to my family—I wish to offer thanks and the hope that this project will enhance our inspiring dialogue together.